Santa's Silly Wishlist

Dear Santa, I would like a skateboard that's rocket-powered so I can zoom to school in seconds!

Dear Santa, can you please bring me a pet dinosaur? I promise to walk it every day (in the backyard)!

Dear Santa, I need an invisible cloak to sneak past bedtime and eat cookies at midnight.

Dear Santa, how about a machine that makes it rain chocolate? Umbrellas would be delicious!

Santa, please could I have a dog that talks? I need someone to argue with my sister.

Santa, can my room clean itself? It's hard to find my bed sometimes!

Hey Santa, a robot that does all my homework would be awesome. More time for cartoons!

Dear Santa, a time machine please! I want to have two birthdays this year!

Santa, a superhero cape that gives me superpowers would be the best. I'll save the world before dinner!

Dear Santa, can you make broccoli taste like bubblegum? That way, I'd eat my veggies every day!

Santa, please can my bed turn into a trampoline every morning? It would make getting up for school so much fun!

I want a cat that glows in the dark, Santa. It would be like having a furry nightlight!

Santa, how about socks that jump into the washing machine by themselves? I keep losing them!

I'd love a book that reads itself out loud, Santa. Especially during bedtime!

Santa, I want a teddy bear that can fly and shoot lasers from its eyes. It would be my super sidekick!

I wish for a flying school bus, Santa. It would be like a magic carpet ride to school every day!

Please, Santa, a hat that makes ice cream appear whenever I'm hungry. It would be the coolest hat ever!

Dear Santa, I'd really like a robot penguin to be my butler. It can waddle around serving snacks and telling penguin jokes!

Santa, can you bring me invisible paint? I want to create secret art that only shows up under a special light!

I wish for a pillow that whispers different bedtime stories every night. It should have a library of adventures!

Please, Santa, can my school be a giant bouncy castle? Learning while bouncing would be so much fun!

Santa, I want a pet dragon that sneezes flowers. It would be the best show-and-tell ever!

Dear Santa, for my last wish, I want a Bedtime Delaying Clock! Every time I say 'just five more minutes, please,' the clock adds five more minutes of playtime before bed.